An Encyclopedia of Animals

Elizabeth Massie

Rigby®

A Harcourt Achieve Imprint

www.Rigby.com
1-800-531-5015

Introduction

   With so many animals in the world, how can we tell the difference between them? One way is to group together animals that have things in common. You will notice that all of the animals in this book have a backbone. You have a backbone, too. It is the bone that runs down your back!

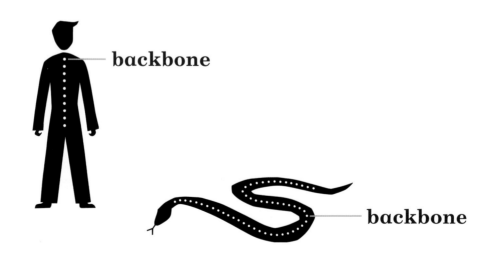

backbone

backbone

Animals with backbones can be mammals, birds, reptiles, amphibians, or fish. The symbols below tell you the group each animal belongs to.

 Mammals

 Birds

 Reptiles

 Amphibians

 Fish

As you learn about these different animals, trace the backbone with your finger.

Alligator

Alligators are large animals with tough, scaly skin. They swim by moving their tails from side to side. Alligators use their sharp teeth and powerful jaws to catch and eat fish, snakes, and other small animals.

Fun Fact
Alligators have between 60 and 80 teeth!

Asian Black Bear

4–6 Feet

Asian black bears have thick black or brown fur with white markings on their chests. Adults can weigh as much as 330 pounds. Strong claws help this bear climb trees in search of birds, honey, and insects to eat.

Catfish

1–2 Feet

Catfish swim along the bottom of ponds or rivers searching for food. A catfish has feelers that look like whiskers on its lips and chin. Because these feelers can taste whatever they touch, they are just like human tongues.

Fun Fact
An upside-down catfish swims upside down!

Eagle Owl

2–3 Feet

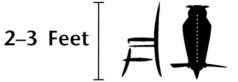

Eagle owls are large birds with orange eyes. They live in rocky places, sometimes in nests built by other birds. Like most owls, these birds rest during the day and hunt small animals at night.

A
B
C
D
E
F
G
H
I
J
K
L
M
N
O
P
Q
R
S
T
U
V
W
X
Y
Z

Frog

2–3 Inches

Frogs are comfortable on land and in the water. Their powerful back legs help them swim across ponds, hop along the shore, and balance on lily pads. A frog catches insects with its quick tongue.

Giant Panda

4–6 Feet

Giant pandas live in the mountains of China, where it is cold. Thick fur coats help keep them comfortable. Pandas like to eat bamboo, but they also enjoy honey when they can find a bees' nest.

Gorilla

Imagine hiking through a forest in Africa and seeing a gorilla using its strong arms to climb a tree! Gorillas like to eat leaves and berries all day long.

Fun Fact

People call adult male gorillas "silverbacks" because of the silver-gray fur on their backs.

Iguana

Iguanas like heat, so they often sit on rocks, sunning themselves. In cooler months, they dig holes in the ground and hibernate. The desert iguana lives in northern Mexico and the southwestern United States.

Japanese Giant Salamander

5 Feet

Because salamanders take in water through their skin, they never need to drink. They have a long, sticky tongue that they use to catch worms and insects. A Japanese giant salamander can grow up to 5 feet long!

Kangaroo

6–7 Feet

Kangaroos are different from other mammals because they hop from place to place on their back legs. A kangaroo's tail helps it balance as it moves over logs, between trees, and across fields.

 # Llama

5–6 Feet

Have you ever wondered whether animals can tell each other what they're thinking? Llamas can! When a llama lays back its ears, it is telling other llamas that it is not happy. A mother llama may also hum to her baby so that it will stay near her.

Fun Fact
When a llama is angry, it may spit!

Mexican Gray Wolf

Mexican gray wolves live in groups, or packs. Birds, mice, and other animals are hunted by these wolves. When wolves howl, they are talking to each other. There aren't many Mexican gray wolves living in the wild today.

A B C D E F G H I J K L M N O P Q R S T U V W X Y Z

15

Newt

4 Inches

Newts hatch from eggs. Young newts live in the water and breathe through gills. Some newts have toes that help them paddle across the water. They swim by quickly whipping their tails from side to side.

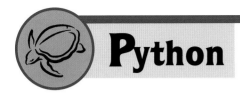

Python

20–30 Feet

You might be amazed at how strong a snake can be! A python wraps itself around an animal, squeezes it, and then swallows it whole. Since pythons eat large animals, such as wild pigs and deer, they only have to eat about once every three weeks.

Fun Fact
This snake swallowed its dinner, then curled up to rest.

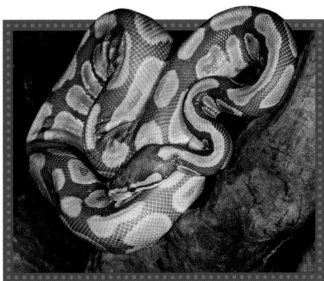

A
B
C
D
E
F
G
H
I
J
K
L
M
N
O
P
Q
R
S
T
U
V
W
X
Y
Z

Quail

8–9 Inches

Quails are birds that scratch the earth with their feet, looking for insects and worms to eat. One common quail is the bobwhite quail. Bobwhite quails build their nests in tall grass for protection.

18

Shark

Many people are afraid of sharks, but only a few kinds of sharks will actually harm humans. Most sharks have several rows of sharp teeth. When some teeth break or fall out, other teeth move forward to take their place.

Toucan

20 Inches

Toucans are birds with long, colorful beaks. Even though a toucan's beak seems too big for its body, it is almost weightless. A toucan uses its beak to pick fruit off tree branches and steal eggs from other birds' nests.

Wagtail

7–8 Inches

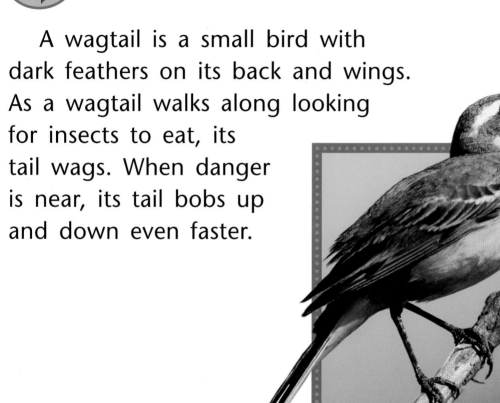

A wagtail is a small bird with dark feathers on its back and wings. As a wagtail walks along looking for insects to eat, its tail wags. When danger is near, its tail bobs up and down even faster.

Water Buffalo

5–6 Feet

Water buffalo live near rivers and lakes, where they eat plants that grow beside the water. Mothers and their babies live together in herds. The mothers protect the babies from danger. Male water buffalo live apart from the herd.

Yelloweye Rockfish

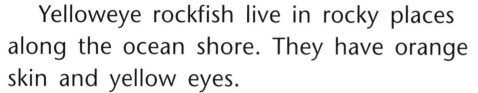

Yelloweye rockfish live in rocky places along the ocean shore. They have orange skin and yellow eyes. Yelloweye rockfish eat shrimp, snails, and smaller fish.

A B C D E F G H I J K L M N O P Q R S T U V W X Y Z

Zebra

Even though a zebra may look like a horse with stripes, it isn't a horse. A zebra is smaller than a horse, with a shorter mane and larger ears. Zebras can see and hear enemies from far away.

Fun Fact

The stripes on a zebra help it hide in tall grass from its enemies.